MW01042987

THE CROSS WALK

JAMES W. MOORE

THE CROSS WALK

A Lenten Study for Adults

ABINGDON PRESS
Nashville

THE CROSS WALK: A LENTEN STUDY FOR ADULTS

Copyright © 1999 by Abingdon Press

This book is printed on acid-free paper.

Library of Congress Cataloging-in-Publication Data

Moore, James W. (James Wendell), 1938–
    The Cross Walk: a lenten study for adults/James W. Moore.
      p.   cm.
    ISBN 0-687-03281-4 (alk. paper)
    1. Lent.   2. Christian education—Textbooks for adults—Methodist.
I. Title.
BV85.M575   1999
242'.34—dc21
                                                      99-31063
                                                           CIP

Scripture quotations, unless otherwise indicated, are from the New Revised Standard Version Bible, © 1989, by the Division of Christian Education of the National Council of the Churches of Christ in the United States of America.

Scripture quotations noted RSV are from the Revised Standard Version of the Bible, copyright 1946, 1952, 1971 by the Division of Christian Education of the National Council of Churches of Christ in the USA. Used by permission.

The story on pages 56-59 is from the article "Nothing can separate us . . ." by Kelly Haugh Clem. Adapted with permission from Guideposts Magazine. Copyright © 1996 by Guideposts, Carmel, New York 10512.

99 00 01 02 03 04 05 06 07 08 — 10 9 8 7 6 5 4 3 2 1

MANUFACTURED IN THE UNITED STATES OF AMERICA

CONTENTS

INTRODUCTION 7

FIRST WEEK IN LENT
Jesus and the Man Who Was Paralyzed 9

SECOND WEEK IN LENT
Jesus and Zacchaeus 18

THIRD WEEK IN LENT
Jesus and the Syrophoenician Woman 26

FOURTH WEEK IN LENT
Jesus and Caiaphas 34

FIFTH WEEK IN LENT
Jesus and Judas 41

SIXTH WEEK IN LENT
Jesus and Pontius Pilate 49

HOLY WEEK / EASTER
Jesus and Mary Magdalene 56

Introduction

Some years ago, a reporter asked the late comedian Flip Wilson about his faith commitment. "Oh, haven't you heard?" said Flip Wilson, "I'm a Jehovah's Bystander."

"A Jehovah's Bystander?" the reporter questioned. "I've never heard of a Jehovah's Bystander. What in the world is that?"

To which Flip Wilson replied, "Well, they asked me to be a witness, but I didn't want to get that involved!"

In his tongue-in-cheek way, Flip Wilson was teasing us, making fun of the way so many people play around the edges of commitment but are afraid to make the leap of faith; afraid to give themselves totally, completely, unflinchingly, wholeheartedly. The season of Lent calls us to deeper commitment and challenges us to examine our faith with questions like these:

- Are we real witnesses or just bystanders?
- Are we as deeply committed as we could be?
- Are we really involved, heart and soul, in living the faith daily?
- Are we really loyal to Christ and his church, supporting the church with our prayers, our presence, our gifts, and our service?
- Can people see the Spirit of Christ in us?

Lent is a call to deeper involvement and deeper faith.

To move us in that direction, let me invite you on a journey, a *spiritual* journey, as we walk together with Jesus to and through the cross in these days of Lent. As we make this journey, we will meet some intriguing personalities along the way:

- The Man Who Was Paralyzed—with the help of his friends, he came through the roof into the presence of Jesus;

- Zacchaeus, the despised tax collector;
- the Syrophoenician woman, whose model of faith and love led to Jesus' act of healing her daughter;
- Caiphas, the scheming high priest;
- Judas, the trusted disciple who betrayed his master;
- and Pontius Pilate, the governor who washed his hands and sent Jesus to the Cross.

But the journey doesn't stop on Good Friday. It continues onto Easter Sunday morning with Mary Magdalene's joyous shout, HE IS RISEN! and with the promise we can claim today as we make our spiritual journey not just through Lent, but through life.

We never walk alone! This is the Good News of Easter. There on Good Friday, at the Place of the Skull, evil had its best chance to defeat God and couldn't do it.

God Wins!

Goodness Wins!

Love Wins!

That's the message of Easter: *God Triumphs*. And God wants to share that victory with you and me. We never walk alone. Jesus is risen! He is with us! He will see us through!

As we begin our journey together, let's see what we can learn from our Master along the way, as we (with him) "set our face toward Jerusalem."

JESUS AND THE MAN WHO WAS PARALYZED

Scripture: **Read Mark 2:1-12**

There is a story about a woman named Denise, who made a routine trip to the grocery store one afternoon—and had an experience there that was anything but routine! As Denise got out of her car in the supermarket parking lot, she noticed something unusual. In the car parked next to her was a woman seated in the driver's seat with her arms draped over the steering wheel, her head resting on her arms, and her eyes closed tightly. She was not moving a muscle; she was perfectly still.

Denise thought to herself, *That's odd. Is the woman okay? Is she in trouble? Is she sick? Has she had a heart attack? Has she fainted? Or maybe she's just resting or sleeping or praying.* Denise wondered whether she should say anything. She finally decided to go into the grocery store and do her shopping and to then check back to see if the situation had changed. Forty-five minutes later, when Denise had finished her shopping, she came back to her car. Immediately she noticed that the woman in the next car was in exactly the same position she had been in earlier and was absolutely motionless, arms draped over the steering wheel, head resting on her arms, eyes closed, not moving at all.

Denise then became really concerned. She went around the car to the driver's side and knocked on the window...no response. At this point, Denise probably should have gone to find a security officer, but wanting so much to help, she opened the door and said to the woman, "Are you all right?"

The woman replied, weakly, "I've been shot! I've been shot in the neck," the woman said. Now, let me quickly tell you that this is going to turn out all right, but at that moment Denise couldn't figure it out, because there were no signs of foul play—no blood, no bullet holes in the car windows.

Denise examined the left side of the woman's neck: nothing. Next she examined the front of her neck: nothing. Denise then went around to the passenger side, got in the car, and looked at the right side of the woman's neck; nothing there, either. Then Denise got on her knees, leaned back over the seat, and examined the back of the woman's neck. There she found not a bullet or gunshot wound, but rather an uncooked biscuit stuck to the back of the woman's neck. Denise looked in the backseat and saw a sack of groceries. At the top of the sack was a can of biscuits, which had exploded and obviously had propelled an uncooked biscuit forward and the biscuit had hit and stuck on the back of the woman's neck.

When Denise told the woman that she had not been shot but rather had been hit by a flying biscuit, the woman didn't believe her at first. So Denise peeled the biscuit off the back of the woman's neck and showed it to her, whereupon the woman straightened up and said thank you, and drove off!

Now, that story is intriguing to me for a couple of reasons. First of all, think of what it says about the violent society in which we live—a world so volatile that when a woman hears a loud pop behind her and then feels a thud on the back of her neck, her first thought is, I've been shot!

But the story also reminds me of the sad fact that there are people in our world today who are emotionally and spiritually frozen like that woman. They feel hopeless and helpless. They have been so hurt by life that they now just stonewall through the days, afraid to move, afraid to act, afraid to live because they believe that they have been mortally wounded. They have no energy, no strength, no zest, no fire anymore. They need someone to come and save them. They need someone to come along and peel the biscuit off the back of their neck and say to them, "Hey! Look! It's not as bad as you think. You are not mortally wounded. You can have a new chance, a new start, a new birth, a new beginning, a new life. There is one who can save you, one who can turn it around for you, one who can heal you."

That's what the amazing story in Mark 2 is all about. Jesus heals the man who is paralyzed and gives him a new lease on life. Now, let me hurry to say that there are many people in our world today with physically handicapping conditions who live full, productive, and meaningful lives. And some of these individuals are more "whole and healthy" than others who perhaps do not have a physical disability and yet are emotionally and spiritually frozen. To be certain, "wholeness" is not merely a measure of one's physical condition. But this man in Mark 2 was not whole. There is evidence to suggest that his problem may well have been more emotional and spiritual than physical. The man's friends were genuinely concerned about him, so in compassion they brought him to Jesus.

Remember the story with me. It was one of those remarkable events in the ministry of Jesus; an event so vivid, so dramatic, so unforgettable that three of the four Gospel writers included it in their narratives. It is such a fascinating incident that it challenges our imaginations to read between the lines and fill in some of the unrecorded details.

We don't know the name of the man who was paralyzed, so let's call him Simon. Simon had been paralyzed as long as people could remember. He was carried around on a straw-filled pallet by his friends. Simon was a familiar sight around town, down by the lakeshore, at the marketplace, in the synagogue. And whenever his pallet appeared, carried by loyal friends, a sigh of pity probably went up from the crowd: "Well, here comes Simon. Poor guy. Bless his heart!" Simon's situation was complicated by a mistaken notion of the time that disabilities and serious diseases were the consequence of some wrongdoing, by the person who experienced them or perhaps by someone in that person's family. For example, if a child were born blind, the immediate response of the community would be to say, *Who sinned? Who caused this?* (Jesus came to refute this idea; the Book of Job also addresses this issue.)

So we can imagine that at first, Simon must have clung desperately to the hope of recovering his ability to walk, trying every physician, every magician, and every faith healer who came to Capernaum, but all to no avail. No one could help him! Each time, each failure to find help would dash Simon's hopes a little more.

But then one day, four friends burst into Simon's home. "Great news, Simon, great news!" they shout. "You can be made well! It is Jesus of Nazareth. He's here in Capernaum. He has helped others; he can help you! Come on, let's go! There will be a big crowd. We must hurry to get in."

No response from Simon. He has heard this before. He has tried so many times before, only to be disappointed. Wearily, he shakes his head and thinks, *There's no use. This Jesus is probably just another fake, another charlatan who will say a few exotic words, make a few mysterious motions, and then take our money and leave town, never to be heard from again.*

But Simon's friends are enthusiastic. "It doesn't matter what you think Simon. The Nazarene is here! This is your big chance, and we are not going to let you miss it. The whole town is over there. We're taking you to see him, even if we have to break our way in."

And that is exactly what they have to do. When they reach the house where Jesus is speaking, they find it surrounded by a throng of people, a solid mass of humanity. There is no way to break through the crowd.

Here they stand, four men carrying their friend on a straw-filled pallet, unable to get inside the building. What to do? For a moment they stand there in stunned silence, the situation seemingly hopeless; they so desperately wanted their friend to see Jesus, and now it looked as if that would not happen. Then one of the friends has an idea: the roof! *That's* the answer! It would be quick work to climb the outside stairs to the door, dig down through the sticks and mud from which the house was built, and then lower Simon right to the feet of Jesus, the Great Physician.

Can't you picture the amazement of the hushed crowd inside the house as they hear the noise above them, and as they look up to see this man being lowered on his pallet down into the presence of Jesus? But Jesus shows no surprise. He is pleased! He is touched by the ingenuity and stubborn faith of these four friends who will not be denied. They so love Simon, and they so believe in Jesus' power to help him that they will not quit! They find a way to accomplish their mission. Jesus' heart goes out to them, and as he sees their faith, he says to Simon, "Son, your sins are forgiven." Jesus tells him he can get up and walk now. And Simon does!

End of story? Happy ending? No, not quite. The scribes and Pharisees are upset with Jesus. They murmur in the background, talk behind his back, and plot against him.

Isn't that a great story? Many things could be noted and examined here. For example, we could look at the relationship between forgiveness and healing: Why did Jesus say, "Your sins are forgiven," as he healed the man who was paralyzed?"

Perhaps we could explore the idea of healing as a story of inclusion. Part of Jesus' ministry of healing was to return people to their community—as he did with those who had a disability or a debilitating illness such as leprosy—to restore their membership and the benefits of being a full, accepted member of the day's society.

Or we could look at the conflict between Jesus and the religious authorities of the day. The watchdogs of orthodox religion became hostile with Jesus for healing the man who was paralyzed, and for the manner in which Jesus did so; why?

All of these issues are important, but for now, let's zero in on the *faith* of the four loyal friends. These men had a great faith, a creative faith, a faith that expressed itself beautifully in service, a faith that said to their hurting friend, "There is hope for you. It's not over. You are not mortally wounded. The Great Physician can heal you—in whatever way you need healing in your life." In the friends' deep faith, we see some of the rare qualities that make the Christian faith and Christian service so special. Let me show you what I mean.

There Is Sensitivity—That Special Ability to See and Seize the Moment

The four friends were sensitive to the needs of their hurting friend, so aware and so sensitive that they didn't wait to be asked for help. They saw the need and responded. Not only that, but they were also sensitive to the specialness of the moment. George Frederick Watt's portrait of the rich young ruler (see Mark 10:17-22) shows nothing but a man's back. You can see disappointment in his drooped shoulders and uncertainty in his fingers and hands, which are half open and half shut. This is the tragic picture of a man who has missed his moment.

Most of the tragic characters in the New Testament are people like that, people who have missed the specialness of their moment: the elder brother (Luke 15:11-32), the one-talent servant (Matthew 25:14-30), the priest and the Levite (Luke 10:25-

37), the foolish bridesmaids (Matthew 25:1-12), Pontius Pilate, Judas Iscariot—all were tragic characters because they missed or mishandled their big moments. But here in Mark 2 we see these men, these four friends who were sensitive enough to see that this was it, this was their big chance to help their friend, and they grabbed it; they seized the moment.

And on top of that, look at the sensitive, thoughtful spirit of Jesus here. One legend regarding this passage holds that the man who was paralyzed had been a stonemason. In this telling, he was a devout man but was forced by Herod to work on the Sabbath. This bothered him. He felt guilty about working on the Lord's Day but was afraid to disobey Herod and the power of Rome. According to the story, the man was injured on the Sabbath and then felt even more guilt. He felt that God was angry with him and that God was punishing him for breaking the fourth commandment. (See William Barclay's *The Daily Study Bible: The Gospel of Mark,* Westminster Press, 1971).

Even apart from this account, the Scripture indicates that the man's paralysis probably was not only physical but also spiritual. Whatever his physical situation may have been, here was a man who was immobilized by the guilt, remorse, and shame that he carried with him, and that's why Jesus, when healing Simon, first told him, "Your sins are forgiven." Jesus met his need, met him where he was, gave him what he most needed. In essence, Jesus had said to him, "It's okay, Simon. God is not angry with you. God loves you, God forgives you. You can have new life. You are not mortally wounded. God is not against you. He is *for* you. He wants to be your friend. You are forgiven. You are made spiritually whole. You are healed."

That's the first thing we notice here: A key ingredient in Christian faith and in Christian outreach is sensitivity.

There Is Perseverance

The four friends refused to give up when they saw that big crowd surrounding the house. They would not quit. They would not be denied. They were totally committed to their task. They were determined to find a way, and they did. Their perseverance paid off. Perseverance usually does. Let me illustrate this.

Sir Winston Churchill took three years just to get through the eighth grade because he had trouble learning English. How ironic and fascinating that many years later, Oxford University invited him to give the commencement address at their graduation exercises.

Churchill accepted the invitation and arrived at the university with his usual props—his cane and his top hat. Those two items accompanied Winston Churchill wherever he went.

When the time came for his speech, Sir Winston approached the podium. He received a standing ovation. With dignity, he settled the crowd and stood confident before his admirers. Placing his cane and his top hat on the podium, Churchill gazed at his waiting audience.

Then came the speech. With authority, Winston Churchill shouted to those students three words: *"Never give up!"* Several seconds passed before Sir Winston rose to his toes and said it again. *"Never give up!"* His words thundered dramatically in the students' ears. There was a deafening silence as Churchill reached for his top hat and cane and walked off the stage. His commencement address was finished. "Never give up!" That was no doubt the shortest and most eloquent commencement address ever given. Yet these are the words that should echo in our hearts and minds each time challenges, problems, or opportunities come our way. (Paraphrase from *The Speaker's Sourcebook* by Glenn Van Ereken, Prentice Hall, Englewood Cliffs, New Jersey 07632; page 276.)

There's no doubt about it. A key component in Christian faith and in Christian service is perseverance. The four friends in Mark 2 would not give up, and they impressed Jesus with their sensitivity and their perseverance.

There is Love

The four friends reached out in love to help their friend, and in love, Jesus did the rest.

G. Steve Sallee tells the story of a woman named Karen. When Karen was expecting her second child, her three-year-old son, Michael, began a relationship with his unborn sister by singing to her every night. Night after night Michael would get closer to his expectant mother's tummy and sing his favorite song to his sister—"You Are My Sunshine."

When the time came for Karen to give birth to the baby, there was trouble during the delivery, and Michael's baby sister was in serious condition by the time she was born. She was rushed to the intensive care unit. As the days crawled by, the baby grew weaker. Doctors feared the worst and began to try to prepare the parents for the baby's expected death.

Meanwhile, little Michael kept asking about his new baby sister. He wanted to see her. He wanted to sing to her. The parents took Michael to the hospital. They put him in a scrub suit and took him into the ICU to see his sister. A hospital staff member who didn't know the situation became disturbed about a three-year-old coming into the intensive care unit and instructed the parents to remove the boy from the area. But Michael's mother said, "He is not leaving until he sings to his sister." Michael walked over to the little bassinet that held his tiny sister. He leaned over the edge and began to sing to her the familiar words of happiness and sunshine that so perfectly described the pure, sweet love he had for her and felt in his heart.

> You are my sunshine, my only sunshine . . .
> Please don't take my sunshine away.

What happened next was unbelievable. The doctors called it a miracle. Karen called it a miracle of God's love. The next day, when they thought they would be planning a funeral, Michael's baby sister got to go home with her parents and her big brother! She was well! She had responded immediately to the familiar voice of her brother. He sang her to life with his song of love. (Thanks to Leonard Sweet for this story. See *Homiletics*, April-June 1996.)

Now let me ask you something: Will you let God sing you back to life? Will you listen to that familiar voice that was speaking to you before you were born? And once you've heard the music, will you sing other people back to life and faith? There's a world of people out there with empty spirits and no hope because they haven't heard the music of God's love for them. Will you sing it? Will you sing the song with sensitivity, with perseverance, and with love?

Study / Discussion Questions

1. The author refers to Jesus as "the Great Physician." Search through the Gospels to find stories where Jesus healed (some examples can

be found in Matthew 8, verses 1-4, 5-13, and 23-27). In what ways did Jesus bring physical healing? In what ways did he bring spiritual healing? Which type of healing are you most in need of right now in your life?

2. From your reading and from Bible stories you have found, what must be present within a person, in many (but not all) cases, before Jesus' healing takes place? Think of a time in your life when you were lifted out of despair or carried along by the enthusiasm or faith of others—friends, family, or strangers. How did they express to you their faith? How were they able to help you overcome the obstacles to your peace and contentment? In what ways did you benefit from their faith?

3. When have you failed to see or seize the moment, missing out on an important or special opportunity in your life? Being as honest with yourself as you can, what kept you from recognizing or pursuing that opportunity? How did this affect your thoughts and actions in later situations?

4. Think of a time when you did see and seize the moment. What did you do differently this time? What was the outcome? In what ways did your relationship with God make a positive difference?

5. In Hebrews 12:1c, the apostle Paul says, "Let us run with perseverance the race that is set before us"; in your own words, what does this mean? Read Romans 12:12; what does it mean to "persevere in prayer"? What happens when we forget to pray or don't feel that we have time for it?

6. What kinds of miracles are most familiar to you? How has God's love worked miracles in your life or in the lives of others you know? In what ways can God "sing you back to life"? What does the "music of God's love" sound like? Where do we hear it, and how can we "sing" it to others?

Focus for the Week

Prayer is a personal means of communicating with God, both talking and listening. Each day this week, make time to meet with God in prayer. Ask God to

• open your eyes to new and existing opportunities;
• help you find the courage to act when the time is right;
• fill you with the determination and perseverance to work through challenges;
• and allow you to be an active part of the miracle of God's love in your life and in the lives of others, through the example of Jesus Christ.

JESUS AND ZACCHAEUS

Scripture: Read Luke 19:1-10

Some years ago, there was a big gala in Hollywood. Fifteen hundred people were present that night. The famous movie star Ann Blyth was the keynote speaker, and she mesmerized the crowd. She spoke eloquently about the power of words. And when she finished she not only received a standing ovation, but almost everyone who heard her that night wanted a copy of what she had said. In her speech was this magnificent paragraph:

> In the beginning was the word...And since then a billion, million words have been spoken. Soft words, hard words, cold words, warm words. There are words that sing and jump and skip and dance—gay words: little girl words. And there are words with fun in their eyes and things in their pockets and their hair mussed: little boy words. There are young words. And wise old words with a glint in their eye. There are words wide-eyed with wonder, warm cuddly words, soft as a baby's feet. And steel words...stinging...cruel blades of words—and sweet words that press their cheek against yours....Words are everything....In a world at the mercy of the word of God, we are at the mercy of our words. (J. Wallace Hamilton, *Still the Trumpet Sounds*, Tappan, N.J.: Fleming H. Revell, 1970; p. 155)

Ann Blyth was right, wasn't she? Words are so important, so powerful, so influential. A word can excite or depress. A word can lift up or push down. A word can make us glad or mad or sad. Words can inspire and brighten our spirits or they can crush and deflate our souls. Words can motivate and encourage or they can smash and kill.

Communication: What a miracle that is! The transmission of ideas and feelings through words—no mystery is greater than that. "In the beginning was the Word." Everything—understanding, friendship, communication with other people and with God—it all begins with a word. We do not live by bread alone. We live by words. And yet the truth is, sometimes our words do get us into trouble. Many of us are prone to that common malady called "foot-in-mouth disease."

I recently came across three illustrations of this problem. Let me share them with you. Some of you have seen the very popular *Life's Little Instruction Book*. It contains a series of short, perky sayings that give helpful advice for living. Brian Bauknight, my friend and fellow pastor, suggested that there should be a companion volume entitled *Life's Little Instruction Book for Preachers*, which could well include the following tidbits:

1. Never insult anybody, but especially not the chairperson of the finance committee.
2. Never begin your sermon with the words "Knock, Knock!"
3. Never wait until the offering time to begin your sermon preparation.
4. And never, ever say, "And, finally" unless you really mean it.
(From a sermon by Brian Bauknight, August 1, 1993)

A second illustration about how our words can get us into trouble came to my desk from Jan Goodsell, formerly of the Associated Press. She made a list of "The World's Worst Questions." Have you ever asked or have you ever been asked any of the following:

1. Will you promise not to get mad if I ask you something?
2. Don't you have any sense of humor?
3. Do you honestly expect me to believe that?
4. Have I kept you waiting?
5. When are you going to grow up?
6. You probably don't remember me, do you? [Preachers love that one.]
7. [And, finally] Are you asleep?

The third illustration is a prayer. I've seen it a number of times over the years. Recently, it surfaced again. It is called "The Prayer of the Realist." Its source is unknown, but the words are relevant. The prayer, obviously written by a "sea-

soned veteran of life," begins with the words "Lord, you know
that I am growing older." It goes on to plead with God to grant
deliverance . . .

- from talking too much,
- from stating strong opinions on every subject,
- from the recitation of endless detail,
- from complaining constantly about recurring aches and
  pains,
- from thinking that we are always right,
- from nosiness and bossiness and self-righteousness.

The prayer then expresses the tongue-in-cheek notion that it is
such a shame to not use all this incredible store of wisdom and
experience the author has accumulated over the years. The
poem concludes with this sentence: "But you know, O Lord,
that when the end comes, I do want to have a few friends left.
Amen."

The point is clear and obvious: Sometimes we talk too much.
Sometimes we say the wrong things. Sometimes we speak
loudly when we would be better served to listen quietly.
Sometimes our words get us into trouble. Sometimes our words
hurt other people. Sometimes our words come back to haunt us.
But, thankfully, there is another side to that coin: Words can be
wonderful, powerful, magical, even miraculous. Words can help
and heal. Words can restore and redeem. Words can soothe and
save.

We see it in the Zacchaeus story in Luke 19. Here we see
Jesus (who is the living Word of God) speaking the most beautiful words in the world. With verbal expression and with body
language, Jesus speaks to Zacchaeus the most powerful and the
most beautiful words ever spoken. What are those beautiful
words? What is it that Jesus is saying to Zacchaeus (and to us)
that is so magnificent? Simply this: You are loved; you are forgiven; and you are needed. Now, what Jesus literally said was,
"Zacchaeus, hurry and come down; for I must stay at your
house today" (verse 5). But what he really said to Zacchaeus
was, "You are loved, you are forgiven, and you are needed."

If you and I were to make a list of the most beautiful words
in the world, those three statements would be at the top of the
list. You are loved. You are forgiven. And you are needed. Think

about that for a moment. Think about the most powerful and most poignant and most moving moments in your life—those precious moments where you felt inspired, encouraged, and motivated—those special moments where you felt included and supported and valued.

If you will think of those special moments in your life when you were touched deep down in your heart and soul, you will probably find that in those moments someone (perhaps a very important person in your life) was saying to you or you were saying to them one or more of these beautiful statements—you are loved, you are forgiven, you are needed. With the Zacchaeus story as the backdrop for our thinking, let's take a closer look at each of these three stirring statements.

You Are Loved

Did you notice in the story in Luke 19 that Jesus went over to that sycamore tree, looked up, and called Zacchaeus by name? What a loving thing to do! Everyone else in town had labeled Zacchaeus. They called him tax collector. They called him traitor. They called him a cheat, a con man, a turncoat. In their minds, he had sold out to Rome because of greed and self-ishness. So they despised Zacchaeus; they rejected him. They called him thief, cutthroat, outcast. They couldn't stand him. They had written him off as a lost cause.

But then along came Jesus. And look what he did! He surprised everybody. He reached out to Zacchaeus with compassion and love. Of all people: Zacchaeus! Not the mayor, not the governor, not the high priest, not the commanding officer, but this lonely outcast tax collector named Zacchaeus. Jesus reached out to *him*.

Why? Was it because the face of Zacchaeus was the most miserable, the most lonely in the crowd? Was it because Zacchaeus was the most needy one in town that day? Perhaps so. Jesus did indeed have that incredible ability to sense and focus in on the one who needed him most in any given moment. But also, I believe that Jesus saw something that day in Jericho that no one else could see. He saw not only what Zacchaeus was, but what Zacchaeus could become.

Jesus looked at Zacchaeus with the eyes of love, not with blind prejudice, not with angry resentment, not with bitter disappointment, but with the eyes of love and compassion. And he saw him not as a label, not as a stereotype, not as a despicable character, but as a human being, as a person of value, as a potential disciple—and as a sinner (to be sure), but one who could be saved.

In essence, Jesus said to Zacchaeus the most beautiful words ever spoken: You are important to me! You are valuable to me! I care about you! I prize you! You are accepted! You are included! You are loved! And listen—that is precisely what Jesus is saying to you and me right now.

A few years ago, I read about a court decision made by a federal judge in Michigan. A picture of Jesus hanging in a local high school had to come down. "It entangles government in religion," the court's opinion stated. It all happened because a senior student filed suit, saying the picture of Jesus violated his civil rights. The student won the case, and the picture of Jesus came down.

But what is really sad about that event is, to me, what the student said later. He said, "I'm an agnostic, and that picture of Jesus made me feel like an outcast." That poor young man. If only he knew what Jesus is really all about. I wish Zacchaeus could talk to the young man and show him how he's got it backwards. Jesus came so we *won't* feel like outcasts. Jesus came to save us from all of that and to say to us the most powerful and beautiful words in all the world. God loves you. You are included. You are accepted. You are loved. That's number one. You are loved.

You Are Forgiven

In 1974, a man named Fred Snodgrass died. *The New York Times* printed the news with this headline: "Fred Snodgrass, 86, Dead, Ballplayer Who Muffed Flyball in 1912." Well, bless Fred's heart. The muffed flyball had happened sixty-two years earlier, but some sportswriter wouldn't let the world forget that Fred Snodgrass had made a mistake in a ball game in 1912. He spelled it out in detail. It was in the World Series. The hitter hit a pop fly. Fred Snodgrass dropped the ball—made an error—which set up the winning run for the other team. The next batter hit a single, the game was over, and Fred's team, the Giants, lost.

What the sportswriter didn't tell us is that after his baseball career was over, Fred Snodgrass moved to California and settled down in Oxnard. He became mayor of that city. He was a banker and a rancher; he raised his children there. Fred was an outstanding leader in that community. The people there loved him, admired him, and respected him.

Evidently the sportswriter had thought that Fred Snodgrass's life had ended in 1912 when the Giants lost the World Series. But it didn't! It was only an episode, just an event. If you make an error in one event, it doesn't have to be the end! You can have another chance. We all fall and stumble and make mistakes but one thing abides: God's forgiveness (from a sermon by Mark Trotter, November 3, 1985).

As much as anything else, this is what the Zacchaeus story says to you and me: You are forgiven. Like Zacchaeus, you may have messed up. You may have sinned. You may have given in to greed and selfishness. And, like Fred Snodgrass, you may have made a mistake or an error. If so, the story in Luke 19 has great news for you: You can be forgiven! If, like Zacchaeus, you will welcome Jesus into your life with faith, he can turn things around for you. He can pick you up and give you a new start. He can wash you clean by the miracle of his amazing grace.

In this story we have the good news of the Christian faith and the most beautiful words in the world. You are loved, and you are forgiven.

You Are Needed

Imagine a high school boy being recruited to play football for Notre Dame. The coach talks with him and his family, and he accepts an athletic scholarship to the school. But by the fourth day of practice, he finds his body bruised by men who not only run as fast as he can, but who weigh forty to fifty pounds more than he weighs. The boy retreats to the locker room, defeated. He showers, dresses, and takes his uniform to the coach. "I can't do it, Coach! I'm not big enough. I'll never make this team. Here's my uniform. I'll leave so you can give my scholarship to somebody else."

The coach says to him, "Son, I recruited you because I believe in you. I saw the stuff in you to make a great athlete and to make this team. I know you can make it, and I'm going to help you. Now quit feeling sorry for yourself and get back on that field."

This is what God says to us when we feel like quitting because the world is knocking us around. "I recruited you. You are a part of my team, and I need you. Now quit feeling sorry for yourself and get back out there with the team, and let's win some games!" (from Ellsworth Kalas, "Windows to the Truth," *Newscope Inspiration,* April 1990 Series).

That's what Jesus said to Zacchaeus that day. You are loved. You are forgiven. You are needed. And that's what he is saying to you and me this day, the most beautiful words in all the world. You are loved, you are forgiven, you are needed.

Study / Discussion Questions

1. Reread Luke 19:1-10. What made Zacchaeus, a "sinner," want to see Jesus that day? Why did he try so hard?
2. What was the importance of Jesus' calling Zacchaeus by name? What effect do you think this had on Zacchaeus? Read Exodus 3:13-15; Isaiah 62:2; and John 10:3-4. What do these verses tell us about God's name and about our names?
3. Hebrews 10:24 says, "Let us consider how to provoke one another to love and good deeds"; what does this mean to you? The author refers to Jesus' special gift for sensing and ministering to the person who needed him the most in any given moment. What can we do to develop these same skills in ourselves? How do we identify those who need us?
4. The people had labeled Zacchaeus a "sinner" and had negatively judged him based on his profession (a tax collector, loyal to Rome). In what ways do we label people (examples: job, appearance, religious affiliation, and so forth)? Why is it hard for us to reach out to people we have a negative view of? What can we do to see people as they really are, and the potential they have to become something new, as Jesus did with Zacchaeus?
5. Zacchaeus had made mistakes in the past, but Jesus gave him another chance. How did Zacchaeus respond? Read Matthew 18:21-22 and Ephesians 4:31-32. What do these verses tell us about forgiveness and giving someone another chance?
6. According to Ellsworth Kalas, God is saying to each one of us, "I recruited you. You are a part of my team, and I need you." What role do you feel God is calling you to play on the team? Read

Ephesians 4:4-6; and 1 Corinthians 12:14-21, 26. Explain these verses in your own words. If Christ is the head of the church and we are all members of Christ's body, give examples of how we can all work together for the good of Christ and the good of the church.

Focus for the Week

Pray these words from Psalm 19:14: "Let the words of my mouth and the meditation of my heart / be acceptable to you, / O Lord, my rock and my redeemer." Think about and work at using your words to show others they truly are loved, forgiven, and needed.

JESUS AND THE SYROPHOENICIAN WOMAN

Scripture: **Read Mark 7:24-30.**

Sometimes it is not so much *what* we say as *how we say it.* The tone of voice is so important!

For example, I once knew a man who could say "let us pray" and make everybody in the room mad. It was his arrogant tone of voice that irritated people. Or think about it this way: A man seething with anger, wild-eyed, vengeful, hostile, out-of-control, waving his clenched fist in the air, screams, "I'll get those rascals if it's the last thing I ever do!"

Now, contrast that with this. A father, playing hide and seek with his children, and with a twinkle in his eye and fun in his voice, says the very same thing: "I'll get those rascals if it's the last thing I ever do!" Same words, but a vast difference in meaning because of the tone of voice.

I am so glad that we have the words of Jesus recorded in the scriptures, but how much better we could understand them if we could hear his tone of voice. That tone was probably one of the main reasons why the little children wanted to get close to him. Obviously, the children didn't understand all of Jesus' words, but they did understand the love and kindness in his voice.

Little children, people who were poor, people who were hurting, people with disabilities, people who were sick, people who were needy. They were all drawn to Jesus, not just by what he said, but by the way he said it. If, by some miracle, we could actually hear Jesus' words spoken in his special tone of voice, then I think we would be able to understand his message better and catch his spirit so much easier.

This is uniquely the case in the perplexing and somewhat disturbing story in Mark 7, where the Syrophoenician woman comes to Jesus for help. Her daughter is sick. The woman has heard about Jesus and his power to heal. So as a loving, concerned parent she comes to Jesus, kneels before him, and asks him to heal her daughter.

Now here is where the story gets tricky. I think the confusion resides in the fact that we cannot hear Jesus' tone of voice. When we look only at the stark words in black and white on the printed page, it does seem, at first glance, that Jesus is being harsh with the woman. He says to her, "Let the children be fed first, for it is not fair to take the children's food and throw it to the dogs" (verse 27).

What in the world does that mean? Well, the word *children* refers to the Jews, the children of Israel, a special people set apart by God. The word *dogs* refers to the Gentiles. We know from the scriptures that the Jews regarded the Gentiles as "unclean" people, and one of the most popular terms of contempt for the Gentiles was the word *dogs*, meaning the wild dogs of the street, the unclean stray dogs who roamed the gutters, the alleyways, and the garbage dumps.

But interestingly, in the original Greek version of this story in Mark 7, Jesus did not use the usual insulting word for *dogs*. Rather, he used a diminutive word that described not the wild, filthy dogs of the street, but rather the little pet dogs of the house, the family's beloved puppies. In the Greek language, diminutives are characteristically affectionate. Jesus took the sting out of the word, and because he did this, the woman realized immediately that she was with a friend (see William Barclay, *Mark*, St. Andrew UK, 1993; p. 179).

Now this woman, being a Gentile, was considered inferior by the Jewish citizenry. Yet she was also Greek, and the Greek people had a particular gift of conversation—a love for banter, discussion, repartee, debate, mental sparring. The woman sensed at once in Jesus' words and tone that he was speaking with a smile, that it was a friendly dialogue, and that help was on the way.

Not only was this Gentile being treated unusually well, but Jesus was also treating her with a respect not often given to women in those days. Men didn't discuss theological issues with women. In fact, women were treated as inferior, as mindless, as things to be used, as chattel to be owned. But here Jesus honors her by including her in a philosophical discussion, the kind that was so important in the Greek world of old.

Leonard Griffith, in his book *Encounters with Christ,* talks about Jesus' deep respect for women. He puts it like this:

> [Jesus] encountered a number of women during his earthly ministry, and his conduct towards them appears all the more remarkable when you remember the inferior status of woman in the first-century world. The hard Roman treated her as a slave or a plaything. The cultured Greek did not regard her as the intellectual equal of any man. Even the devout Jew listed her as an item of property along with his fields and cattle and would never break the law by talking to her about religion.
>
> The coming of Jesus invested womanhood with a new honor and motherhood with infinite sacredness. Towards women of all races and ranks, even fallen women, Jesus displayed a gallant courtesy, a knightly chivalry, for which he has been well named "the greatest Gentleman of the ages." (New York: Harper & Row, 1965; page 58)

It's no accident that this incident in Mark 7 occurs where it does. Only a few verses earlier, Jesus has shown that there is no distinction between clean and unclean foods. Here in this story, he is showing that there is no distinction between clean and unclean people. Jesus is showing that he came not just for the Jews, but for the Gentiles as well. He is showing that he is not just the Jewish Messiah, but that he is the Lord of Life; the Christ for all people; and the Savior of the whole world. The Gentiles too are included. They too have a place in his kingdom. And aren't we glad of that?

In Mark 7, the Syrophoenician woman realizes that Jesus is befriending her, and she skillfully rises to the occasion with a brilliant response. In essence, she says this: "I know that the children are fed first, but surely I can have the crumbs under the table that the children have thrown away" (verse 28, paraphrased).

Jesus loved the woman's response. He liked her spirit. Hers was a sunny faith that would not quit, a persistent faith that would not take "no" for an answer. Here was a mother with a sick child at home who was willing to take a chance and go out on a limb for the sake of her child.

When tested, she responded with grace and grit, with charm and insight. And Jesus was impressed. He liked her. He liked her boldness and her commitment to her child. And he answered her prayer. "You have answered well," he said to her, "And now you may go your way because your daughter has been made whole" (verse 29, paraphrased).

The woman quickly returned home and found that her mission had been accomplished. Just as Jesus had said, her daughter was completely healed. The illness was completely gone. Jesus had indeed made her well!

This is a fascinating story; and at this point, we could go in a number of directions with it. We could look at the power of Jesus to heal; or we could examine the impact of the Syrophoenician woman's bold persistence; or we could talk about how, as a Greek, she symbolizes all the Gentiles and their inclusion in God's kingdom.

But let me simply invite you to look with me at the poignant portrait of love painted here. In this woman's encounter with Jesus, we see three of the most important ways to express love.

Love Can Be Expressed with Words

The Syrophoenician woman came to Jesus that day to express in words her love for her sick child. Also, don't miss this: In the entire Gospel of Mark, she is the only person who lovingly calls Jesus "Lord" (Mark 7:28).

It seems as though it should be easy to express our love with words, but the truth is that precious few people do that well. Why is that? Why do we have trouble speaking the words of love? If we only realized how powerful words are, I think we would work harder at the task of expressing our love with words.

Some years ago, an older woman was dying in a local hospital. She was in her mid eighties. Her son came by airplane to be with her. I happened to be present when he arrived and entered the room. He walked over to the bedside of his aged and dying mother. He leaned over and kissed her on the cheek. Then, touched by that tender moment of seeing her so weak and vulnerable, he said to her, "Mom, you have been such a good mother to me. And I want you to know I love you."

And through tears, she said to him, "Son, that's the first time you've ever told me. Last Friday was your sixty-third birthday, and that's the first time you've ever told me." It had taken him sixty-three years to say "I love you" to his mother.

Let me ask you something. Is there a word of love you need to speak today? Those of you fortunate enough to still have living parents, how long has it been since you told your mother or father how much you love them and appreciate them? Or how long has it been since you told your mate? I don't mean a quick, routine, matter-of-fact "I love you," but a real heart-to-heart expression of your love in words.

Well, parents, how about you? How long has it been since you told your children how proud you are of them and how much you cherish them? Let me suggest something. For one week, write down every word you say to your children and then ask: How many of these words are words of love, encouragement, and appreciation rather than merely words of correction or discipline? I know that as parents we sometimes have to be referees, and this can be a loving thing to do. But we also need to be cheerleaders. We need to say, "I love you."

There is no question about it. One of the best ways to express love is with words.

Love Can Be Expressed with Attitude

We can express our love with our attitude toward life. One of the things about the Syrophoenician woman that most impressed Jesus was her attitude. She was committed to her child, and she was willing to do whatever it took to get help for her sick daughter. She was bold, persistent, and courageous because she lived by the attitude of love. She would not be put off. She would not be discouraged. She would not give up, because she lived by the attitude of love.

Some years ago in a mining town in West Virginia, a seventeen-year-old boy took a summer job in the coal mines. Being a coal miner for the summer sounded adventuresome and macho. However, the second week on the job, he got lost deep down in the mines. He had been working with a group of veteran miners. They had warned him. They had cautioned him. They had told him to stay close to the group, because it would be so easy to get lost down there in the numerous caves and treacherous passageways of the mine. But the boy had absentmindedly wandered away from his work team and had become lost —completely lost!

He screamed for help, but the miners had moved on to another location, and no one could hear him. Then suddenly, his light went out and he was in total darkness. He was absolutely terrified. He began to cry. He thought to himself, This is how it all ends for me. I'm going to die down here. I don't know which way to go. I don't know how to get out.

The boy dropped down on his knees to pray: "O God, help me!" he said out loud. "O God, please help me!" Then he noticed something. As he was kneeling there to pray, he felt his right knee touching something hard. He felt it. It was a railcar track. He realized that if he kept his hand on that track and followed it, it would lead him out!

That's just what he did. He held onto the track and followed the track, and eventually it brought him out of the dark, out of the depths of the mine, and into light and safety.

That's a parable for us, isn't it? If we will hold onto love and follow wherever it leads, if we will make love our attitude in life, no matter how dark some moments may be, that love— God's love—will bring us out of our darkness and lead us into the light.

As "cliché-ish" as it may sound, it is still profoundly true: *love is the answer!* We would do well to hold on to that track and to live by that attitude. As Christians that is our calling, to live always by the spirit and attitude of love. We can express our love with words and with attitude.

Love Can Be Expressed with Actions

The Syrophoenician woman in Mark 7 put her love to work. She acted it out. She expressed her love with actions. How important that is!

I recall a young woman with whom I attended college. The members of her family were not Christians, and she had not been raised as a Christian. When she had been in high school, she had gone one night to a youth program led by a Methodist college student. That night she was converted. She accepted Christ as her Savior and dedicated her life to Christ.

But then she had a problem. How would she tell her parents about her newfound faith? She decided to not tell them in words, but rather to show them in deeds of love. Here's how she described what happened. She said, "Before Christ came into my life, I was spoiled and selfish. I was irritable and impatient. I was disrespectful to my parents. My room was a mess, and my attitude was worse. But after Christ came into my life, I changed. I was kind to my parents. I cleaned up my room. I helped with the housework. I spoke to my parents with tenderness and respect. I was loving toward everyone. My parents noticed, and they said to me, 'You are different! Why? What has happened to you?' I said to them, 'Yes, I am different. I have been reborn! I have Christ as my Savior. I am a Christian now, and Christians always live by the law of love.' And my parents said, 'Tell us more of this religion. Tell us more of this Christ. If he can change people like that, we want to be Christians too!'"

That's the way it works. As the Syrophoenician woman showed us through her encounter with Jesus, we can express our love with words, with attitude, and—most powerfully, most dramatically, most meaningfully—with actions.

Study / Discussion Questions

1. Try to describe how you imagine Jesus' voice sounded: serious and solemn? inviting and laughing? powerful and commanding? In what ways does Jesus speak to you? Who does most of the talking and who does most of the listening—or is there an even, two-way dialogue?
2. Reread Mark 7:24-30. Why do you think Jesus responded to the woman in the way he did? Could he have made the same point as forcefully but in a different way? How?
3. In Mark 7:28, the woman's response is indicative of her great faith. What other people in the Bible displayed such faith, and how? (You may use your Bible to find examples.) What people in the world today display such faith, and how? In what ways has your faith been tested, and how did you respond?
4. Respond to this question: "Why do we have trouble speaking the

words of love?" Is telling someone you love them sometimes better than showing it? Why might this be true?

5. Read 1 Corinthians 13:4-7 and answer the following questions: In what ways is love expressed in one's attitude? in one's actions? Give specific examples from your life or from the lives of others you know.

Focus for the Week

Think about all of the ways in which you express yourself, and try to see yourself the way others might. Can people tell by your words, your attitude, and your actions that you are full of love for God and for your fellow human beings? Read Matthew 22:37-39, and pray for yourself and others that "Christ may dwell in your hearts through faith, as you are being rooted and grounded in love" (Ephesians 3:17).

JESUS AND CAIAPHAS

Scripture: Read Matthew 26:58-68.

Caiaphas was the high priest at the time Jesus was crucified. The Bible indicates that he was highly responsible for Jesus' death. In fact, in his book *Personalities of the Passion* (Abingdon Press, 1943; pp. 40-46), Leslie Weatherhead dramatically says that more than any other human being, Caiaphas was responsible for putting Jesus on the cross. Listen to Weatherhead's powerful words.

> When we come to Caiaphas, we are getting nearer the forces of evil which drove Jesus to the cross. If the guilt can be laid upon one [person], then that one is not Judas or Pilate, but Caiaphas. To my own mind Judas misunderstood, and Pilate...was frightened; but in Caiaphas there is cool, calculated cunning. There is bitter, implacable hatred. No hot impulse swayed Caiaphas, no grievous misunderstanding, no mere sudden fear. Here is the cold, deadly, clever brain.... Caiaphas is the personification of all that is despicable and foul in the insincere ecclesiastic [or politician].
>
> It is strange that in modern sermons we hear so much about Peter's supposed denial and Judas' alleged wickedness, but...the real villain in the Passion drama...was undoubtedly Caiaphas.

Our scripture lesson only touches upon Caiaphas's place in the story of Jesus, but he was without question a dominant player in that dramatic crescendo of events that led to Golgotha and the death of Jesus on the cross. It is very likely that Caiaphas (and his father-in-law, Annas) orchestrated the whole thing—the arrest, the trial, and the Crucifixion. It is very likely that earlier, when the Gospel writers speak of people plotting to put Jesus to death, Caiaphas was in the dead center of the plotting, conniving, and scheming.

Earlier in the ministry of Jesus, certain people were spying on him, closely watching his every move, and trying to trap him with loaded questions. It is very likely that these spies had been sent out by Caiaphas in search of an excuse—any excuse—to silence Jesus. It is also very likely that Caiaphas and Annas were getting rich through the heavy taxes they had levied on the people (taxes which were, by the way, in addition to the burdensome Roman taxes). In that day, the people on the street talked openly and grudgingly about the greed and corruption and luxurious living of Caiaphas and Annas.

It is very likely that Caiaphas was the one most responsible for turning the Temple into yet another means of bilking the people out of still more money, causing Jesus to become so incensed at this blatant exploitation of the people that he overturned the money changers' tables and remarked that they were turning the Temple into "a den of robbers" (Matthew 21:13). It is very likely that Caiaphas was the one who devised the plan to let the Romans kill Jesus, as well as the plan to actually get him into Roman hands.

And it is also very likely that Caiaphas was the one who whispered into the ear of Pontius Pilate the insidious words, "If you let this man go, you are not the friend of Caesar. We have no king but Caesar." It is likely that Jesus had Caiaphas or someone like him in mind when he said of the religious leaders of his day, "You cleanse the outside of the cup and leave the inside filthy; you mind the small matters of the law and neglect the weightier things like justice and mercy and faith" (Matthew 23:23, 25, paraphrased).

It is likely that in everything Caiaphas did, he had three things uppermost in mind:

1. to protect and feather his own nest;
2. to keep Rome happy; and
3. to hold on to his position as high priest.

After all, he had been appointed to that post not by the Jewish people but by Rome, and he remained in office only by Rome's choice.

It is very likely that Caiaphas had sold out. At this point in his life, he seems only to want to do Rome's bidding, to keep the people quiet, to keep the waters from being stirred up, and to hold on to what he has. And, most frightening of all, it is very likely that when Caiaphas started his career he was a good man, full of idealism and hope and sincerity.

I'm sure that at the beginning, Caiaphas wanted to be the priest of God, the servant of God, the spiritual leader of God's people. But somehow he had lost it. Somehow, Caiaphas had lost his way, lost his early dreams, lost his original motivation, lost his sense of ministry. He had become a wily politician, a schemer for power, an insecure victim of greed, until he was God's high priest in nothing but name.

The story of Caiaphas sends a warning flare into our lives. It shows us in a backdoor sort of way how good people can slowly but surely lose their way and choose comfort over commitment. Let me be more specific. The story of Caiaphas reminds us dramatically (and frighteningly) of three temptations that constantly haunt us—three temptations that constantly threaten us. Let me list them.

The Ever-Present Temptation to Choose Position Over Purpose

Somehow over the years, Caiaphas had lost his purpose. He simply had no purpose in life now except to hold a position that appeared important. He succeeded in this and held the office of high priest for eighteen years.

Generally, those who held the position of high priest did so for only a few years at the most. Rome demanded men who were submissive, who had no ideas of their own and no purpose but to be Rome's puppet. And though Caiaphas may well have begun his priestly career with the highest motivations and the best of intentions, he ended it with no purpose other than simply to remain in place, to hold his position, to guard and protect his nest—comfortable, noncontroversial, secure, but purposeless.

This reminds me of something someone said many years ago about a former President of the United States. A critic of that President said this: "The problem with him was that he didn't want to be President; rather, he wanted to *have been* President." That is, he wanted the honor but not the pressure.

In the 1992 Jurisdictional Conference, one of the retiring bishops said something that fascinated me. As he reflected on his life as a bishop, he quoted Mark Twain, who once said, "If you carry a cat home by the tail, you will learn some things you just don't get in books." Now, why did the bishop quote that in his retirement speech? What did he mean by that? I think he meant that being a bishop is more than an honor. It's hard work, with lots of long, hard meetings; lots of hard, agonizing decisions; lots of wearisome travel; lots of keen responsibility; and lots of intense pressure. Being a bishop is indeed a high honor, but more than that it is a ministry. The bishop is indeed an official, a leader, but more than that the bishop is a servant.

The story of Caiaphas warns us of how easily it can happen—how easily we can be tempted to choose honor over hard work, position over purpose.

The Ever-Present Temptation to Choose Safety Over Service

Many people these days seem to be confusing the notions of safety and service. They mistakenly believe that being saved means playing it safe. Nothing could be less biblical than that.

Caiaphas, when he tried to silence Jesus, was concerned about "playing it safe," survival, safe-guarding his own place. The rich young ruler was trying to find real life, eternal life, but missed it that day because he was playing it safe (see Matthew 19:16-30; Mark 10:17-31; Luke 18:18-30). Simon Peter's most embarrassing moments came in those times and places where he tried to play it safe. Judas Iscariot's betrayal of Jesus may well have been the direct result of his trying to play it safe. And when Pontius Pilate washed his hands, he too was obviously playing it safe, trying to keep his distance, telling himself he wasn't responsible for Jesus' death.

On the other hand, the most truly "saved" persons in the Bible are always those men and women who are "laying their lives on the line," risking their lives for some great dream or commitment. For example, here is Moses, leaving the comfortable, secure, pastoral life of Midian to risk his life for the freedom of his people (see Exodus 3–4).

Here is Deborah, heroic leader of early Israel, bravely facing a fearsome adversary and sacrificing her own personal welfare for her people (see Judges 4–5).

Here is Jeremiah, seeing his nation gone astray and braving

the jeers of the crowd risking all to do what he strongly believes to be the will of God (see the book of Jeremiah).

And here is Jesus, armed with nothing but goodwill and love, standing up to the powerful authorities of his own people and standing up to the awesome might of Rome, surrendering every source of safety and security, striking a blow for justice, and trusting only God for the outcome!

Somehow, Caiaphas had lost sight of why he had become a priest. He had forgotten how to risk, how to care, how to serve. He only knew now how to play it safe. He had become the servant of the bureaucracy rather than the servant of God and his people.

Some time ago, the phone rang one night at the parsonage. I answered it and heard on the other end of the line the sweet voice of an older woman. She said to me, "May I please speak to Martha?"

I responded, "I'm sorry, there is no Martha here."

Click—the phone was abruptly hung up. Then the phone rang a second time. The same light voice, "May I please speak to Martha?"

"I'm sorry, there is no Martha here," I said.

Quickly, another click, and the phone was hung up. Then the phone rang a third time. It was the same soft voice again saying, "May I please speak to Martha?"

As nicely as I could say it, I responded, "I'm terribly sorry, but there is no one here named Martha, and I do believe that you are dialing the wrong number."

To which she replied, "Young man, I am not dialing the wrong number, you are answering the *wrong phone!*"

This is what happened to Caiaphas, isn't it? Somewhere down the line, he started answering the wrong phone—the phone of safety rather than service. And if we are not very careful, that can happen to us. We can tragically choose position over purpose and safety over service.

There Is the Ever-Present Temptation to Choose Convenience Over Christ

How quickly (like Caiaphas) we can forget the whole point of faith! How easy it is to see ourselves as privileged people rather than servant people. We live today in a "cater culture" where we expect to be waited on, and consequently we go through life and through the church saying, "What's in it for me? Who will serve me? Who will cater to me? Who will pamper me?" So quickly we forget the cost of discipleship. So quickly we forget that our symbol is a cross and that we are first and foremost servants.

And so we serve the church—*if* and *when* it's convenient. We attend church—if and when it's convenient. We go to Sunday school—if and when it's convenient. We sing in the choir or work with the children and youth—if and when it's convenient. This was precisely Caiaphas's problem, and it is here more than anywhere else that the spirit of Caiaphas slips into our lives. We ignore the way of the cross and opt instead for the way of convenience. Frederick Buechner, in his biblical Who's Who called *Peculiar Treasures* (Harper & Row, 1979) has a fascinating way of depicting Caiaphas:

> The high priest Caiaphas was essentially a mathematician. When the Jews started worrying that they might all get into hot water with the Romans because of the way Jesus was carrying on, Caiaphas said that in that case they should dump him like a hot potato. His argument ran that it is better for one man to get it in the neck for the sake of many than for many to get it in the neck for the sake of one man. His grim arithmetic proved unassailable.
>
> The arithmetic of Jesus, on the other hand, was atrocious. He said that Heaven gets a bigger kick out of one sinner who repents than out of ninety-nine saints who don't need to.... He said that the more you give away, the more you have.
>
> It is curious that in the matter of deciding his own fate, he reached the same conclusion as Caiaphas and took it in the neck for the sake of many, Caiaphas included. It was not, however, the laws of mathematics that he was following (p. 19).

Caiaphas chose convenience. Christ instead chose suffering, yet in that suffering he brought salvation and freedom from sin and suffering for each and every one of us.

So what's it going to be—position or purpose? Safety or service? Comfort or commitment? Convenience or Christ? Which will *we* choose?

Study / Discussion Questions

1. How do "good" people lose their way—their sense of purpose—and what are the warning signs? Who is to blame—the individual? family members? friends? society? Is there a way in which we can help? How? How might prayer and Christian fellowship make a difference?

2. Jesus, condemning a number of the scribes and Pharisees for their corrupt practices, told them, "You cleanse the outside of the cup and leave the inside filthy" (Matthew 23:23, 25, paraphrased). What do you think Jesus meant by this? How was Caiaphas, the Jewish high priest at the time of Jesus' crucifixion, guilty of this practice? How are we?

3. The author says, "Many people these days...mistakenly believe that being saved means playing it safe. Nothing could be less biblical than that." Look through the Gospels to find examples of Jesus and the disciples choosing service over safety. In what ways has God called you to serve and, in doing so, to ignore what would usually be considered "safe"?

4. What are some ways in which we choose convenience over Christ? Read Matthew 7:13-14. What does this passage tell us about the Christian way of life?

5. Throughout the Sermon on the Mount (Matthew 5–7), Jesus calls each of us to action—to follow his example and set ourselves to the work of making a positive difference in the lives of others. Scan Matthew 5–7 and name some of the requirements of Christian discipleship that Jesus has set out for us. Using these as guidelines, what areas of your life do you feel called to improve upon right now?

Focus for the Week

The author uses the story of Caiaphas to show that as human beings we all face temptation, and that even "good people can slowly but surely lose their way." A troubled life doesn't always involve a sudden, drastic turn for the worse; decay happens in small increments, a little at a time. This week, think privately about specific ways you can recognize and overcome the temptations you face in your life. Read the Bible and speak to God in prayer for guidance in making wise decisions, as you strive to let God's word be "a lamp to your feet and a light to your path" (Psalm 119:25, adapted).

JESUS AND JUDAS

Scripture: Read John 13:21-30.

In the early 1600s, the Black Plague ripped across the globe, killing people by the thousands. In London alone, more than 150,000 persons died from this horrid disease. Then in the year 1633, the Black Plague invaded the beautiful village of Oberammergau, Germany, in the Bavarian Alps. In a short period of time, the plague took the lives of most of the inhabitants of that quaint little mountain village. Driven to desperation, the villagers made a vow to God. They took an oath that they would stage a performance of the Passion of Christ every ten years if the plague vanished.

And the story goes that from this moment on, the village was spared from the black death. No more lives were snatched away by the plague. Whether the feared disease suddenly ended cannot be proved; but in any case, the epidemic was checked. The villagers of Oberammergau believed that God had heard their cry, and they kept their promise. One year later, in 1634, the first Oberammergau Passion Play was presented. The promise to God was fulfilled for the first time in 1634, and since then it has been kept faithfully for more than three and a half centuries.

The play depicts the story of what is known as Christ's Passion, beginning with Palm Sunday, Jesus' triumphal entry into Jerusalem, and on through the arrest, trial, crucifixion, and resurrection of Christ. The performance lasts an entire day. It begins at 9:00 in the morning and concludes at 5:00 in the afternoon, with a three-hour midday lunch break. All the performers are natives of the little village. Their talent is remarkable, their commitment is incredible, and their play has become one of the most beloved in the world.

A few years ago, I had the privilege (along with some close friends and five thousand other people) of experiencing the Oberammergau Passion Play. The entire dramatic presentation was spectacular, but for now I want to focus on their portrayal of Judas, the Betrayer. It was fascinating to me. It was a very sensitive, compassionate portrayal of Judas. It appealed to me because Judas was shown as a character, not just a caricature. That is, he came across not just as a symbol of evil, but as a person (like you and me); as a human being, as a man who got confused as we get confused, who got scared like we get scared; who got taken advantage of like we get taken advantage of; who got stampeded like we get stampeded, only later to shrink back in horror at what he had done—at what he had caused.

The play shows vividly what the scriptures tell us about Judas and yet what we often miss, namely that the tragedy of Judas was not just that he betrayed his Master, but that he stopped too soon! Trouble came, and he didn't persevere; he didn't work through it. You see, we learn from Judas—in a backdoor sort of way—how *not* to handle trouble.

Trouble came, and Judas threw up his hands. He got confused and scared, and he threw in the towel, not realizing the magnitude of his decision, not realizing that the people he was dealing with wanted to kill Jesus. Then, when the weight of what he had done fell upon him, Judas couldn't live with it (Matthew 27:3-5). He quit too soon, turned away too fast, sold out too quickly. And consequently, he never knew the benefits that come from getting to the other side of trouble. Instead, he stopped in the middle. And because Judas stopped too soon, he never knew resurrection. He never knew the strength and power and wonder of the Resurrection.

Isn't that the temptation we all face when trouble comes—to stop too soon, to become scared and panicky and confused, and to quit on our commitments? But when we stop too soon, we miss the strength and new life that comes from going through trouble and getting to the other side.

Of course, none of us likes trouble. We all dread it, but it is inevitably here to be dealt with. In the "Peanuts" comic strip, Lucy issues an ultimatum to our troubled world. She declares, "By the time I'm eighteen, I expect this world to be perfect! Why should I have to live in a troubled world, a world somebody else has messed up? I'll just give them twelve years to get everything in order!"

"But what if they need more time?" asks Charlie Brown.

Lucy retorts, "Tell them not to bother wiring for an extension! The answer will be no!"

But life just doesn't work that way, does it? Trouble is not scared away by insecure ultimatums. Trouble is a universal experience; it is something all of us know. And the real issue is how you handle it, how you deal with it when it comes. One woman, who was disabled after an accident, said to her family, "I'll show you how to take trouble. How you take it is the only thing about it that's important."

This may well be the real tragedy of Judas. He couldn't handle his trouble. Trouble was brewing. Just think of it; tensions were crackling in the air. The events, the groups, the pressures, the confrontations, the personalities that were coming together in Jerusalem were ticking like a time bomb, ready to explode at any moment. Maybe it was too much for Judas. Maybe he cracked under the pressure. Judas had been a devoted follower of Jesus for many months. He had been liked, respected, and trusted by the other disciples. They had chosen him to be their treasurer. In Galilee, all had gone well.

But then came that significant moment when Jesus set his face toward Jerusalem. He came to Jerusalem bringing his followers with him, walking right into the middle of trouble, right into the heart of the storm. He had one confrontation after another with the Pharisees, the Sadducees, and the high priests. In addition, Roman soldiers were all about, and hostility was building against Jesus and his followers. Trouble was in the air. It was in the very air they breathed.

And perhaps Judas got scared and confused. He had heard Jesus talk about a Kingdom, but now, all of a sudden, he was talking about a cross. This was not what Judas had in mind. The Sadducees likely sensed his panic, and they moved in on him. Before Judas realized what was happening, he was taken in. And in his fearful, perplexed state of mind, he sold out. He betrayed his Lord. He stopped too soon, pulled up stakes too quickly, and consequently he never knew the strength that could have come from holding on, working through, and getting to the other side of trouble. Many people, like Judas, make the tragic mistake of quitting too quickly, of stopping in the middle of their trouble and thus missing the new life on the other side.

A few summers ago, our family was vacationing in the Great Smoky Mountains. While we were there, we kept hearing people talk about a gorgeous mountain drive nearby with a breathtaking view. One afternoon we got directions and launched out in search of this much-talked-about view of the Smoky Mountains. But to tell you the truth, we didn't see anything that was spectacular. We saw a lot of little tourist shops on the side of the road with birdbaths and corncob pipes and peacock blankets, and that was about it. So we returned to the hotel that evening a little disappointed that our drive hadn't been more exciting.

Later that night we were having dinner with some friends and they said, "Now, before you leave, we must take you up on a mountain drive to see a sight so spectacular that you will never forget it." We were puzzled and finally confessed that we had been up there that very afternoon and had not seen anything so exciting. Then they asked, "How far did you go?" And when we told them, our friends said, "That's the trouble. You turned back too soon. If you had just gone on over the next ridge, you would have seen a sight there that's so breathtaking you could never forget it in a lifetime. From that point, you can see a hundred miles or more in every direction."

You see, our problem was that we stopped too soon. We had no idea what was on the other side of the ridge.

On the other side of trouble is strength and new life; Judas stopped too soon, and thus he never discovered that fact. Let me suggest some strengths and benefits that come from working through our troubles and getting to the other side.

On the Other Side of Trouble Is a New Understanding of Life, A New Perspective of What Life Is All About

When you get to the other side of trouble, you realize that burdens do come, but they also go. Troubles do come, but they also pass. Sometimes when you are in the midst of a problem, you are down in the valley and you can see no way out. You feel like the trouble is here forever and you will never get out of it. But you will. You will get to the other side, and when you do, you will realize that it didn't take so long after all. The trouble did pass, and you did get through it.

I was thumbing through some of our family photo albums in the den one evening when I came upon some pictures of our daughter, Jodi, made when she was two years old. I was reminded of something that happened to her at that age. She was climbing on the couch in our living room when she toppled over the back side of it and landed on her ankle, spraining it pretty badly. We rushed her to the emergency room. The doctor diagnosed the sprain, wrapped her little ankle, and told us to keep her off of it for a few days. Jodi told everybody that her foot was broken, and even after several days, she made no attempt to walk. Even when we would encourage her, she made no effort, and there was no indication that she would ever walk again.

Finally, we talked to the doctor. He checked Jodi and assured us that the ankle was completely well, and that there was no reason why she couldn't walk by now. "Encourage her," he suggested. We tried and tried, but nothing worked. She simply refused to even try to walk. Finally, one evening, we took Jodi to a toy store and put her down in the aisle, in the midst of all the toys. Excitedly, she began to run from one toy to another, and when she realized what she was doing—that she was walking and running—she suddenly stopped, looked down at her feet and turned to us. With a surprised expression, she said, "Look! I can walk, I can walk!"

At that moment, we realized that we had failed to communicate to her that she was going to recover, that she would get over it, that she would get well. The only experience she had had with broken things was with her dolls, and when they were broken, they were broken forever, never to be fixed again. Jodi had the idea that she would have a sprained ankle for the rest of her life. Of course, she was mistaken. Healing came in time.

You know, we are like that sometimes with our troubles. Sometimes we feel that they will never be over. But they will. Time passes, and things heal. The tragedy of Judas was that he saw no way out of his problems. He didn't realize that God, in his own time and in his own way, could bring healing and forgiveness, yes, even to Judas.

On the Other Side of Trouble Is a New Strength to Help Others;
A New Empathy, a New Compassion, a New Witness

Some years ago, I was called to the hospital to visit a young couple who had just lost a baby, one day old. I felt very inadequate for the task. What do you say in a situation like that? I had a prayer with them and tried to say something consoling, but I knew they weren't really hearing a word I was saying. They just sat there in stunned silence. But then there was a gentle knock at the door. It was D. L. Dykes. He came in. He took their hands, and the first thing he said to them was, "Did you know that some years ago, my wife and I lost a baby too?"

All of a sudden their eyes seemed more alert, and their faces seemed brighter, and they listened closely as he comforted them. They were hanging on his every word. And he helped them so much more powerfully than I ever could have. I was amazed at the power he had because he had walked through that valley of sorrow. He had been there, and that gives you a power and strength that is indescribable—and so beautiful. When you have passed through trouble and reached the other side, you have a new strength to help others.

On the Other Side of Trouble Is a New Faith,
A New Relationship with God

Have you read the book *The Hiding Place*? There's a movie version, as well. It's the story of Corrie ten Boom and her family, a Dutch family, who lived in Holland during World War II. They were a Christian family who tried to help the Jewish people escape the wrath of the Nazis. They were eventually captured by the Nazis and put in concentration camps where their faith was sorely tested. In fact, Corrie ten Boom was the only one in her family to survive the prison camps. She lived to tell of it. And she lived to tell that she knew that God was with them.

The theme of that book is caught up in a phrase repeated several times in the story, namely, "There is no pit so deep that God is not deeper still." That's what we discover as we work through our troubles. That God is with us, and that there is no pit so deep that God is not deeper still.

On the Other Side of Trouble Is a New Ability To Turn Defeat into Victories

Isn't that precisely what Christ did—turn defeat into victory? Isn't that what the cross is all about, taking bad things and turning them into good things; taking defeats and turning them into victories; taking the "downs" of life and turning them into "ups." Think about it. Jesus faced the worst troubles the world can dish out. Poverty came his way; temptation came his way; criticism was poured out upon him; false rumors were started about him; he was misunderstood and mistreated. He was betrayed by one of his followers, forsaken by his friends. He was mocked, he was taunted, he was beaten. He was crucified.

But Jesus took those troubles and redeemed them and used them for good. And he turned them into victories! He took that crown of thorns and that cross and turned them into symbols of love and triumph. And the good news of our faith is that by the grace of God and with God's help, you and I can do that too! To do less is to stop too soon.

Study / Discussion Questions

1. The author describes Judas not as a caricature of evil, but as a flawed human being. Think about Judas, the person. Why do you think he was chosen to be an apostle? What characteristics do you think he possessed that led him to be chosen as the apostles' treasurer? What does the author say was the real tragedy of Judas?
2. Describe a time in your life when you gave up, failed to see a situation through, or didn't work through your troubles. What was the result? Were you seeking God's guidance at this time in your life? In what ways was God guiding you?
3. Read Hebrews 2:17-18 and Hebrews 4:15-16. How is Jesus able to offer us a special help and understanding—a new perspective—when we are tempted and face trouble? Now read Isaiah 40:31. What does this passage tell us about the healing power of God?
4. Read Luke 22:32; Romans 15:2; and 1 Thessalonians 5:11. What are the central messages of these verses? Think of a time when you were able to help others as the result of suffering or difficulties that you had faced. How did you offer your counsel or assistance? How did God use you to do God's good works?
5. In your own words, rewrite or explain this statement: "There is no pit so deep that God is not deeper still." How is our faith changed

and our relationship with God made new through our suffering and
our struggles?

6. Through his crucifixion and resurrection, Jesus turned the defeat of
death into the victory of eternal life. From your own life or the
lives of others, give some examples where God's grace was at work
to turn defeat into victory.

Focus for the Week

To persevere means to have enduring patience, to "persist or remain
constant to a purpose, an idea, or a task in the face of obstacles or dis-
couragement" (American Heritage Dictionary, 3d ed.). And for
Christians, our purpose is to follow the example of Jesus Christ in loving God and loving others.

This week in your prayers, share with God your burdens, your
struggles, your fears, your sorrows—everything that is weighing heav-
ily in your mind and on your heart. Ask God to open your eyes to a
new understanding, to deepen your faith, to give you the strength to
help others, and to impart to you the ability to turn your defeats into
victories. And most of all, ask God to give you the perseverance you
need to get to "the strength and new life that comes from going
through trouble and getting to the other side."

JESUS AND PONTIUS PILATE

Scripture: Read Matthew 27:15-26.

Jesus came riding triumphantly into Jerusalem on Palm Sunday, the picture of success. But then, just a few days later, he was nailed to a cross like a common criminal. What happened? What do we make of this? Was Jesus a success?

For many years now, Americans have been highly success conscious, and in fact, success oriented. And most have agreed with one of Webster's definitions: success is "the gaining of wealth, fame . . . ." Think about it. Isn't it true that when we think of success, we immediately recall names such as Rockefeller, Kennedy, Ford, DuPont, or Trump. They symbolize the "sweet smell of success." But Webster was wrong. Money and fame are not enough. In fact, some who *look* highly successful are actually quite miserable.

Some years ago, a well-dressed young man came to a priest in Paris for counseling. He complained of being blue, unfulfilled, and depressed. The elderly priest said to the young man, "Go to Grimaldi! He is the handsome, young, happy-go-lucky leader of the Continental jet set. He is the life of every party. His frivolous good times are legendary all over Europe. He is known far and wide for his joyous exploits. The whole world envies Grimaldi." Then the priest said "go to Grimaldi. He will show you how to be happy."

"But sir," said the young man, "I am Grimaldi!"

You see, there is more to successful living than partying, being in the limelight, and counting wealth. Our customary standards of measuring success are so flimsy and shallow. "How much money do you make?" "How many cars do you have?" "When was the last time you had breakfast in Paris, my dear?" The questions we ask reflect a poverty of the soul and a gross misunderstanding of what genuine success is really all about.

What is the other side of success? Well, think about Holy Week and that dramatic scene in the Gospels where Jesus stands before Pontius Pilate. What a contrast! How different these two men are! Notice something here. If you asked people today who knew nothing of the story to point out the successful one in this scene, using our present-day standards for measuring success, many would quickly point to Pontius Pilate. The folks probably would support their choice by underscoring Pilate's wealth, his position, his power, his authority, his political clout, his fame, and yet they would be wrong! So very wrong!

In Jesus, we see an entirely new and different understanding of what success is. His approach is so different that it startles us. In effect, he says, "If you want to be great or successful, then be a servant" (see Matthew 20:20-28).

"Be a servant?" What on earth can Jesus mean by that? "Successful people aren't servants. Successful people *have* servants!" we cry out. What is he trying to do here, upset our whole scale of values? Well—yes! That is precisely what Jesus is trying to do, to give us a new scale of values, a new measuring stick, a new standard for measuring success.

Now, with that as a backdrop, let's look together at some of the qualities of life that seemed of great importance to Jesus, the qualities that make for real success. Here is number one.

Real Success Is Not So Much in Outer Circumstances as It Is in Inner Stability, Inner Peace, and Strength

Look again at the scene in Matthew 27:15-26 in light of this idea. Who has the inner peace and strength here? The outer circumstances favor Pilate, but not the inner stability. Jesus is the strong one here. In fact, his inner strength baffles Pilate.

Pilate is confused, upset, weak. He can't make up his mind. In a dither, he runs from one group to the other, asking questions here and there. He tries to pass the buck. He knows that Jesus is innocent, but Pilate does not have the strength of character to stand firm for what is right. This is the picture of a man who is "running scared." Outwardly he has it all—power, wealth, position, fame. But inwardly, where it really counts, Pilate is scared to death. Finally, he washes his hands, tries to straddle the fence. Nervously, he gives the people what they want—he turns Jesus over to them for execution—but then, just in case someone else may see it differently, he tries to act as if he is not really involved. Let me ask you something: Is that success? Is being scared, confused, and weak "success"? Surely not!

On the other hand, look at Jesus! He stands there poised, confident, and unafraid. He is facing death, but his strength never wavers. Just think of it: an unfair trial for an innocent man; lies; plotting; conniving; bribed witnesses; political intrigue; jealousy; hostility; hatred; a mob scene; and in the face of it all, Jesus exhibits an amazing quality of inner peace and strength and calm. They betray him, deny him, taunt him, beat him, curse him, spit upon him and nail him to a cross, and he says, "Father, forgive them; for they do not know what they are doing" (Luke 23:34). Now, that is strength of character, isn't it? That is inner peace. That is real success.

Real success is not so much in our circumstances as it is in inner stability. And in that regard, Jesus was the most successful man who ever lived.

But how lacking are these qualities of peace and inner strength in our world today? People chain smoke, knowing the consequences, because they are nervous within. People become habitual drinkers, knowing the consequences, because they are restless within. People drug themselves, tranquilize themselves, because the mounting pressures of life have torn their inner world to shreds. Some people would give anything for a good night's rest, for a sense of peace within. Jesus offers it to us. "Peace I leave with you; my peace I give to you" (John 14:27a).

This, for the Christian, is the source of calm and inner strength. It was the contagion of this confidence that enabled those early Christians to stand unflinchingly against horrible persecution, to sing hymns of praise in prison cells, and to face death with courage and poise. Their inner lives were strong, secure, peaceful. Their inner lives were successful, and that is the only success that really matters. Real success is not out there; it's in here!

Real Success Is Not So Much in Having Many Possessions As It Is in Pursuing a Dream

Real success lies in giving your life *to* and *for* something bigger than you. A dream, a cause, a purpose, a ministry—these are more important than all the money and all the material possessions in the world.

I once visited a successful businessman in his luxurious office suite. It was magnificent, elegant, perfectly and expensively furnished. The man showed me into his private office, closed the door, and said, "Jim, I have everything I ever dreamed of having, and more. I have wealth, power, authority. I have a fine home, three luxury cars, money to do anything I want to do. I have a lovely wife, wonderful children, a respected career, and I am in good health. But despite all that, I am miserable. I feel empty inside, unfulfilled. I am bored to tears! People call me a success, but I feel like a failure." Now, what that man was saying was that he has everything but a cause, everything but a dream. And without that, his life is an empty shell.

When *Man of La Mancha* opened on Broadway in November of 1965, there was not much excitement about it. Nobody expected much from the production. It was only another staging of the Don Quixote story, the story of a man fighting for a cause he believed in. The opening night audience came, not expecting much, not overly excited. But when the final curtain came down, the audience, as one, rose to a resounding, roof-raising standing ovation. The people cheered, shouted, applauded—some were moved to tears. The critics raved, calling it a musical that would last for generations. Why? Because the words and music tugged at something buried deep down in the human heart, something that most people thought to be dead and gone forever. It was the appeal of a great dream, the challenge of striving after some tremendous ideal.

Jesus knew about that important longing deep within us, and in the Sermon on the Mount, he underscored it by saying, "Strive first for the kingdom of God and his righteousness, and [everything else] will be given to you as well" (Matthew 6:33). "Blessed are those who hunger and thirst for righteousness, for they will be filled" (Matthew 5:6).

Patrick Henry, American statesman and orator, knew the importance of pursuing a great dream. He closed his will with these words:

> I have now disposed of all my property to my family. There is one thing more that I wish I could give them and that is the Christian

faith. If they had this and I had not given them one shilling, they would be rich; and if they had not that and I have given them all the world, they would be poor.

Success does not come from material possessions. Success comes from giving your life to a great dream.

Real Success Is Not Living for Self; It Is Living for Others

A little boy came home from Sunday school. He had studied the parable of the good Samaritan. The boy's mother asked him, "What did you learn?"

He said, "I learned that when I'm in trouble, somebody ought to help me!"

Well, it's good that he learned *something!* But unfortunately, he missed the point. And too often, so do we.

By our present-day standards of success, Jesus wouldn't measure up so well. He was born in a stable. His mother was a peasant girl, his father a carpenter. Jesus had little formal schooling, wrote no books, held no public offices, claimed no political fame. He traveled very little. He taught, but many scoffed at his teaching. His closest friends betrayed him. And then, almost before his story even got started, Jesus was nailed to a cross like a common criminal and put to death.

That doesn't sound like a success story, does it? And yet two thousand years later, people bow at his name and look in amazement at his perceptive teaching and his sacrificial death. People's lives are changed because of him! Why? Because he showed us what God is like and what God wants us to become, and the word is *love.* Jesus said that the one who is to be the greatest and most successful among us must be a servant—a servant of God, of people, of love (see Matthew 18:15; 20:26*b*-28; Mark 9:33-37; Luke 9:46-48).

Some years ago, a group from our church toured China. One Sunday morning, we had the privilege of worshiping in a Christian church in Guilin, China. It was packed with worshipers. We came to church unannounced, and the people accepted us warmly in the Spirit of Christ. The minister preached a three-point sermon in Chinese, and though we couldn't understand all of what he was saying, we got the drift of it. He was lifting up Jesus Christ as the Lord of life and the Savior of the world.

Then, after the sermon, we stood and sang the closing hymn, "More Love to Thee, O Christ, More Love to Thee!" Think of it. There we were, twelve thousand miles away, singing that familiar hymn with that gracious and welcoming Chinese congregation. Some of us were holding our hymnals upside down, but we were singing it together powerfully. And it dawned on me in a fresh, new way, the incredible impact of Jesus Christ on this world!

So if you want to be a success, accept Christ into your heart as your personal Savior and know the inner strength that comes from that. If you want to be a success, catch hold of his dream and commit your life to that dream. If you want to be a success, live every day—every moment—as a servant of Christ's love. That's what it's all about.

Study / Discussion Questions

1. According to the author, Pilate's actions and decisions during Jesus' trial and sentencing were motivated by his being "scared, confused, and weak." When you experience these feelings, how do they play themselves out in your actions and decision making? Read Psalm 23; John 14:27; and 2 Corinthians 13:11. What do these passages tell us about inner peace and calm and where to find it?
2. Explain this statement: "Real success is not out there; it's in here." How do we know whether we are successful? How can we tell whether someone else is successful?
3. The author says that a dream, a cause, a purpose, and a ministry are all more important than money and possessions. Do you agree? Give some examples that show this to be true. Think about and then try to answer this question: What is your dream, your cause, your purpose, or your ministry?
4. The Gospels show a number of examples of Jesus being a servant, including his washing the apostles' feet at the Last Supper (John 13:3-5); healing on the sabbath, even though forbidden by law (Matthew 12:10-13); and feeding a large crowd of hungry people who had come to hear him preach (Matthew 14:13-21). What was Jesus trying to show us with these acts? What does being a servant mean to you? How can we be the kind of servants Jesus is calling us to be?

Focus for the Week

Some say that the things that are the most important to us are those on which we spend the most time. Being as honest with yourself as possible, rank your current priorities in life, such as family; friends; work; property (house, car, money); technology (computers, the Internet); recreation, entertainment, and leisure (sports, movies, music, vacations, rest or sleep); self-improvement; community service; church; worship; prayer; Bible study; and any other categories that you can think of. What do you think your list says about what you value or believe is important? How much time or energy do you spend on yourself? on others? What changes, if any, do you feel you need to make?

JESUS AND MARY MAGDALENE

Scripture: Read John 20:11-18.

In March of 1994, the Reverend Kelly Clem was pastor of the Goshen United Methodist Church in Piedmont, Alabama. Kelly and her husband, Dale, had two children: Sarah, age two, and Hannah, age four. Four-year-old Hannah was a delightful character, so full of life and love and enthusiasm. Just a few days before Palm Sunday, Kelly picked up Hannah at preschool. As they drove home through the Alabama countryside, Hanna got so excited about the incredible sunset—purple and pink, her favorite colors. "Look, Mommy, look!" she shouted, bouncing up and down on the seat. At times, it seemed the word *exuberant* had been invented just to describe little Hannah. The smallest things exhilarated her—pine cones, rainbows, colorful leaves, the way an owl's head turns all the way around. She never saw a tree she didn't want to climb, or a rock she didn't want to carry home. She was that kind of child. Exuberant, enthusiastic, loving, lively.

As the car pulled into the driveway of the parsonage, Hannah asked a childlike question: "Mommy," she said, "will we die at the same time? Will you and Daddy and Sarah all die at the same time?"

Kelly was startled by the question at first. What had brought that on? Was it the tornado drill Hannah's school had practiced earlier in the week? "Well," Kelly answered gently, "we may not die at the same time, but I believe we'll all be together again."

Hannah accepted the answer quickly, and then she said, "When you die, you get buried. Then you go live with God."

As they climbed out of the car, the conversation hung in Kelly's mind like a cloud. But Hannah was already back to the splendors of being a child, and she began picking up pine cones to take to her friends next door. Hannah loved to give away her treasures—the rocks in her pocket, the colorful leaves, the pine cones, and the rainbows she had painted at preschool.

When Palm Sunday came, Kelly Clem stepped into her pulpit. The church was packed, filled to capacity with 140 worshipers. Two-year-old Sarah was in the nursery. Four-year-old Hannah was dressed up in her blue and white robe, sitting on the front pew with the children's choir. She was grinning at her mother. Kelly's husband, Dale, was away on a mission trip in Oklahoma.

The service started, it was to be like no other. Rain was falling outside, pelting the windows. Lightning and thunder crackled and shuddered. The lights flickered. There was the sound of hail hitting the south wall of the church. People turned and looked. A baby near the back cried out. Then suddenly, a stained glass window on the south side shattered, spewing purple and white glass across the sanctuary. "Get down," someone screamed from the front of the church, "it's a tornado!" Pieces of the ceiling started to fall. It seemed as if the whole world were exploding. The roof lifted off the building and then crashed down.

Kelly ran out of the pulpit, trying to get to her children, but a flying brick hit her on the side of the head. She fell hard on her shoulder. She covered her head as chunks of concrete and bricks and glass were coming down from everywhere. Then it was over. Kelly pushed away the rubble around her and was able to stand. Others struggling to their feet, calling out to loved ones. There was devastation everywhere. Hannah and Sarah! Where were they?

Kelly looked back toward the nursery. That part of the church was still standing. Someone at the back held Sarah up, letting Kelly know that she was all right. Kelly worked with others to free those trapped beneath the beams and blocks. Then she saw it. A piece of blue and white material protruding from a pile of bricks beneath the first pew. It was Hannah. They pulled her out, but it was too late. Hannah Clem and nineteen others died that Palm Sunday morning; eighty-six more were injured, many severely.

In the days that followed, the funerals were held. The church family was devastated by the disaster, so much so that Kelly

Clem, as their pastor, wondered if the church could survive this. Could they find the strength to go on? She wondered if she could find the strength to go on. Kelly, so stunned with grief and pain, could not at that moment see any future for that little church.

But then the phone began to ring. Church members wanted to know if there would be an Easter service. These were the same people who had lost loved ones, people also in great grief, people who had been injured. Kelly knew that they were thinking about what had happened to Jesus on the cross—what had happened to them and their church and their loved ones—and they were longing for Easter. They needed Easter. "Yes," Kelly said, "we will have a sunrise service right on the lawn beside the church. We'll be out there at dawn waiting for Easter."

Kelly thought to herself: What in the world am I going to say? On Thursday morning, Kelly had her answer. She woke up with a scripture passage repeating itself in her head. She knew that God had given it to her and that God meant for her to read it to the people on Easter morning. Kelly's heart was broken and her hope was battered. But those words of scripture touched something deep down inside her and resurrected her; they brought her back to life.

On Easter Sunday morning, Kelly and two hundred other worshipers gathered in the predawn darkness. In the center of the ruins where the altar had once been, someone had erected a large wooden cross. Then at exactly 7:00 A.M., when Kelly stood to begin the service, the sun spilled over the horizon in purple-pink colors Hannah would have loved. With her face swollen and her shoulder in a brace, Kelly stepped up to the makeshift podium. "I can't think of any other place I'd rather be," she said, "Can you?"

Kelly opened her Bible and read the words God had given her: "Who shall separate us from the love of Christ? Shall tribulation, or distress, or persecution or famine, or nakedness, or peril, or sword?... No, in all these things we are more than conquerors through him who loved us. For I am sure that neither death, nor life, ... nor things present, nor things to come, ... nor anything else in all creation, will be able to separate us from the love of God in Christ Jesus our Lord" (Romans 8:35, 37-39 RSV). When Kelly read this passage, she looked out into that sea of faces and saw the people nodding, with tears in their eyes. She knew then that they would indeed go on. A year later, they had rebuilt their church in the shape of a butterfly—a symbol of rebirth and resurrection.

In July following the tornado, Kelly, Sarah, and Dale went out into their backyard to remember Hannah's birthday. She would have been five years old. They stood on the stump of a tree that had been destroyed by the tornado. They held seven helium-filled balloons, each a different color of the rainbow. They let them go one-by-one, and as they did, they celebrated something special about Hannah's life, her exuberance, her delight in small things, her zest for life, her love that compelled her to give away her treasures. They recalled her words she had spoken about death just a few days before she died, and her simple faith that God is good and life with him follows death. As the balloons sailed away, Kelly said she felt that Hannah was teaching them the things they needed to be able to go on. It was as if God was reminding them, through Hannah, to have a simple but pro-found threefold approach to life—to live deep, to love much, and to have faith. (See *Guideposts*, April, 1996, pp. 2-7; and also Dale Clem, *Winds of Fury, Circles of Grace*, Abingdon Press, 1997.)

Isn't that precisely what Easter is trying to teach us? Isn't that what Christ taught throughout his earthly ministry? Isn't that what he died for—and rose again to underscore? Isn't that what Mary Magdalene discovered on that first Easter morning when she came and found an empty tomb and a Risen Lord? Storms come, heartaches come, Good Fridays come. But they are always followed by Easter Sunday mornings! Please don't forget that, because Easter is too precious to miss or to waste.

The key to life is to remember the good news of Easter, the good news that nothing can defeat God, that nothing can separate us from the love of Christ—not tornadoes, not death, not anything. And knowing that, trusting that, we can—by the grace of God and because of the miracle and reminder of Easter—live deep, love much, and have faith. Let's take a closer look at each of these.

Easter Reminds Us to Live Deep

The late "Pistol" Pete Maravich was one of the greatest basketball players who ever lived. Many of his basketball records still stand today. But Pete Maravich led an unsettled, empty, shallow life until he met Jesus Christ. In his book, *Heir to a Dream* (Thomas Nelson, 1987), Maravich reflected upon the powerful transformation that had occurred in his life and in the life of his dying father, for whom he had so lovingly provided care until the end:

> As I watched my dad getting more sickly each day, I prayed for a miracle.... Then I realized the real miracle had already happened. The miracle is the amazing growth our relationship underwent because of our faith in Jesus. [Dad's] illness drew us close, but the love we shared in Christ drew us closer than I ever believed possible.
>
> I always knew that my Dad and I had a very special relationship; he was not only my father and coach, he was my friend and confidant. We shared the same dream, the same passion in life, but our dream had only brought us sorrow. All the fame and fortune the dream had promised left us as empty men until the day we received Jesus Christ into our hearts. At that point I became more than an heir to a dream, I became an heir to salvation and so did Dad.

On another occasion, Maravich shared this message with a group of 17,000 young people in North Carolina:

> In the past if someone had offered me a million dollars, I would've chosen it and celebrated because of all the things I could do and all the things I could have. I've never known anyone who would turn down a million bucks. But, on the other hand, God has been trying to give eternal life, totally free, and most people have rejected the offer, saying, "I'll take the million."

But Maravich told the crowd that finding God and coming to Christ had changed him, changed his outlook and his priorities.

> The feeling of total emptiness is no longer there. Money can buy you everything but happiness. It can pay your fare to everywhere but heaven....
>
> [I]f you seek pleasure and happiness you'll never find it. But if you have the wisdom and obedience to seek Jesus Christ, happiness will find you.

That's what Easter teaches us—that life in Christ is the most valuable and most important thing in the world. And when we realize that and accept him in faith, we are on our way to living deep.

Easter Reminds Us to Love Much

Have you heard the story about a little boy named Richard who grew up in a family of nine children? Richard was the youngest. When he was seven years old, he was asked by his mother one Saturday night to come upstairs and polish her shoes. There were so many children to get ready for bed and to get ready for church the next day, and she needed help.

Richard was glad to help his mother, and after a short time, he brought in her Sunday shoes, all clean and shiny. He was so proud of what a good job he had done. His mother too was pleased and delighted. To show her appreciation, she reached into her purse and gave Richard a quarter. That was big money back then, and Richard was a bit puzzled. He took the quarter, picked up his mother's shoes, and carried them back to her room.

The next morning, Richard's mother rushed to get ready for church. As she put on her left shoe, she noticed a lump in the toe of the shoe. She took the shoe off and found a wad of notebook paper. As she unfolded the paper, a quarter fell out! There on the paper, in a seven-year-old's scrawl, were written these words: "I done it for love!"

Richard's grammar needed work, but his heart was right. Already at age seven, he knew about a special kind of love called *agape*—unconditional love, love that gives graciously, love with no strings attached, love that is self-giving. That's what Christian love is all about. Jesus showed us that over and over in words and deeds. Jesus showed us that on a cross. And when he came out of that tomb on Easter morning, he showed us that love is the most powerful thing in the world. Spires always outlast spears because spires are made out of love and for love. Easter reminds us to live deep and to love much.

Easter Reminds Us to Have Faith

Mary Magdalene came to the tomb that first Easter morning defeated, in deep pain and grief and despair. She came shaken and hopeless. But look—she leaves running and shouting the faithful cry of Easter. "I have seen the Lord! He is risen! I have seen the Lord!" Mary realized that morning that nothing can defeat God and that nothing can separate us from the love of Christ, not even death. There is no grave deep enough, no stone big enough, no army strong enough, no seal tight enough to keep Christ in the grave. If that doesn't thrill us and touch our hearts, then we need to check our spiritual pulses!

One of the warmest memories of my childhood was something that happened to me when I was five years old. I had spent the day with my grandmother. Toward evening, a fierce storm hit. "Oh, Jim," my grandmother said, "how in the world are we going to get you home in this weather?" The answer came moments later as my dad walked in the front door. He had come to get me. The storm showed no signs of letting up. The wind was blowing hard, rain was pelting down, lightning was flashing in the sky, thunder was rumbling behind the clouds.

It was a dark and scary night. We didn't have to go far to get to our house, but the storm was nasty and getting worse. Dad had on a big blue all-weather coat, and as we got ready to leave my grandmother's, he said, "Son, come under here." He covered me with his coat, and out into the storm we went. Even though it was raining hard and the wind was howling and I couldn't see a thing under that coat, I was not afraid at all. Why? Because I knew my father could see where we were going. So I just held on tightly and trusted him. Soon the coat opened, and we were home.

Death is like that, I think. Grief is like that too. God covers us with his protective love. He holds our hand and guides us through the storm. Sometimes there is no way around it. We have to walk through the hard Good Fridays of life, the storms, the pain, the heartache. But the good news of Easter is this: We never walk alone. Christ is risen. He is with us. He will see us through!

Study / Discussion Questions

1. Describe a "storm" you have experienced in your life. How were you able to get through it? What comfort did you find during this difficult time? Describe what it was like when the "storm" subsided and the "daylight" broke through.

2. Describe what it means to you to "live deep." What are the outward signs of a deep life? What are the inward signs? How do God and your relationship with God fit into your idea of a deep life?
3. The author says that "spires [like church steeples] always outlast spears because spires are made out of love and for love." What are some ways in which the church today shows or encourages agape—unconditional love? How can the church improve in this area? What can you do to better show agape in your own life?
4. Mary Magdalene was one of Jesus' most faithful disciples; she was present at his crucifixion, was the first to find his tomb empty on Easter morning, and was the first person to whom Jesus revealed himself after his resurrection. Reread John 20:11-18; try to imagine yourself in Mary's place at these events, and describe the thoughts and feelings she must have had. How does the good news of Easter—that Jesus Christ has risen from the dead and has gone on to God to prepare a new life for us there—strengthen and transform your faith?
5. Take just a few minutes to think about or discuss the time you have spent during this Lenten season in study, discussion, and prayer. What have you learned and experienced in your walk with Jesus? In what ways have you grown and changed? How has your relationship with God and with others been enriched? How can you help others to have faith, live deep, and love much?

Focus for the Week

As you celebrate the glory and triumph of the Resurrected Christ this Easter, look back upon the road Jesus took to get here—his "cross walk"—and ask yourself these questions: Where are you in your walk with Jesus? Where have you traveled, and where are you headed?

Jesus' message to each one of us is simply this: Love God, and love others. This week and every week, today and every day, let this message guide you in your walk. And even through the valleys, even through the storms, you'll never have to walk alone: God is walking with you, each step of the way!